Where in the World is WOOLLOOMOOLOO?

Bill Condon

Where in the World?

Mars is in outer Space – right? Well, yes, but there's also a place in the USA called Mars – as well as a town called Earth! Canada has towns called Cat Guts and Horse Chops. In Ireland there's Horse and Jockey, in Australia there's Wangi Wangi and in Germany there's Rottenegg. And where in the world do you think you would find Cow Head and Mosquito?

Cow Head and Mosquito are in Canada!

Let's find out about some places with weird and wonderful names!

The study of place names is called **toponymy**, and that's what we'll do right now!

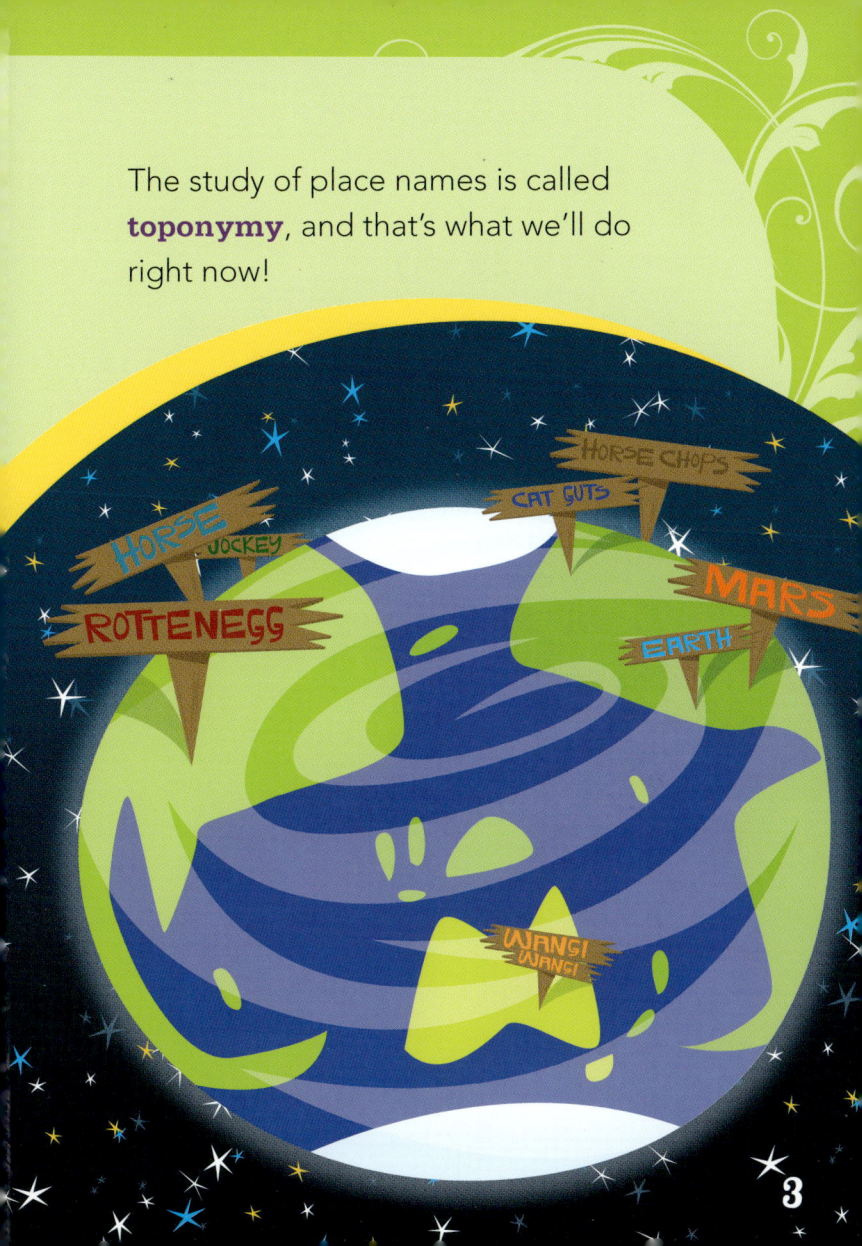

Place Names — Weird, Wacky and

What's in a Name?

How some places get their names

PAGES 6 TO 9

Wish You Were Here!

Postcards from the oddest places

PAGES 10 TO 11

Where Am I?

I think I'm confused . . .

PAGES 12 TO 13

Wonderful!

Say What?

How on Earth do you say these names?

PAGES 14 TO 15

Very Strange Names!

These may be the weirdest names in the world!

PAGES 16 TO 21

What's in a Name?

Many place names are very old. They come from the people who first lived in an area. **Early names** often described the place. In England and Scotland a 'dun' was a hill, an 'aber' was a river mouth and a 'combe' was a deep valley. The words 'ham', 'thorpe', 'tun' and 'by' meant farm or homestead. Place names ending in 'burgh' meant that they were ancient fortresses.

This place is in a deep valley. What could it be called?

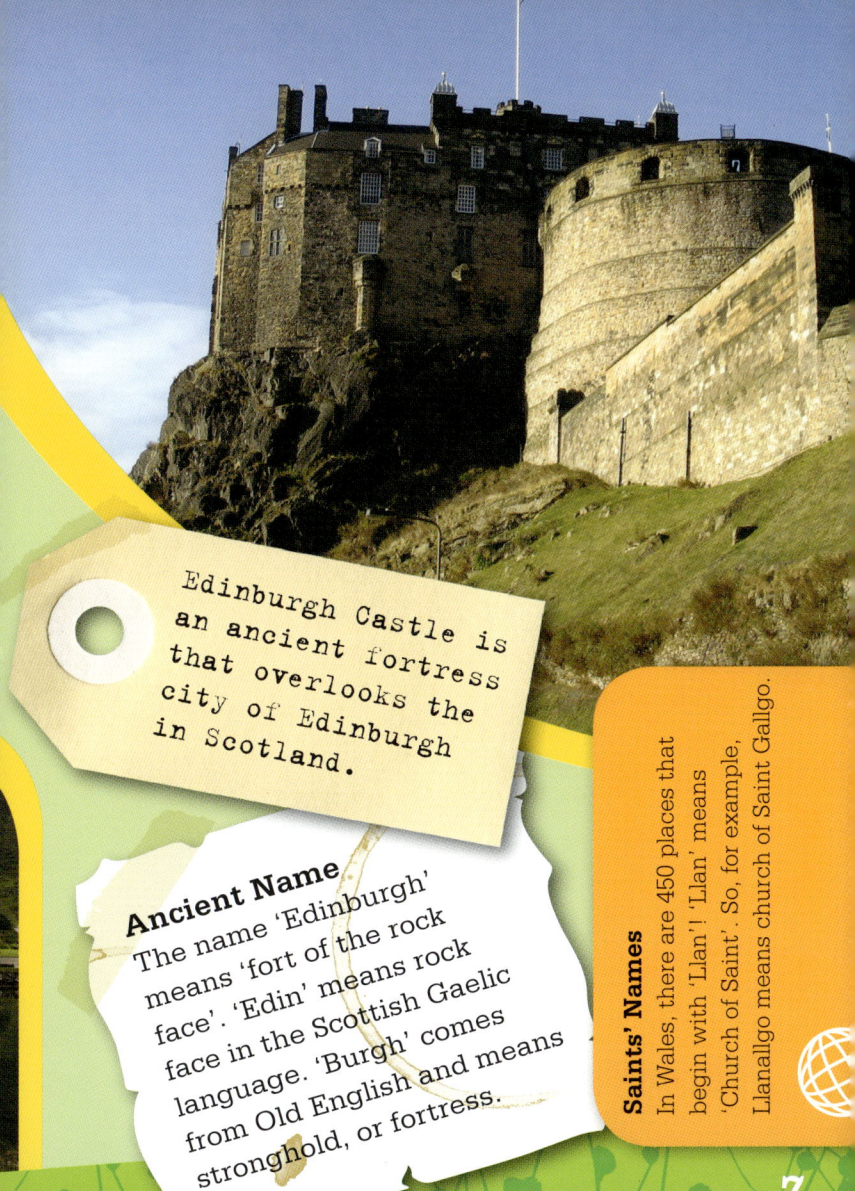

Edinburgh Castle is an ancient fortress that overlooks the city of Edinburgh in Scotland.

Ancient Name

The name 'Edinburgh' means 'fort of the rock face'. 'Edin' means rock face in the Scottish Gaelic language. 'Burgh' comes from Old English and means stronghold, or fortress.

Saints' Names

In Wales, there are 450 places that begin with 'Llan'! 'Llan' means 'Church of Saint'. So, for example, Llanallgo means church of Saint Gallgo.

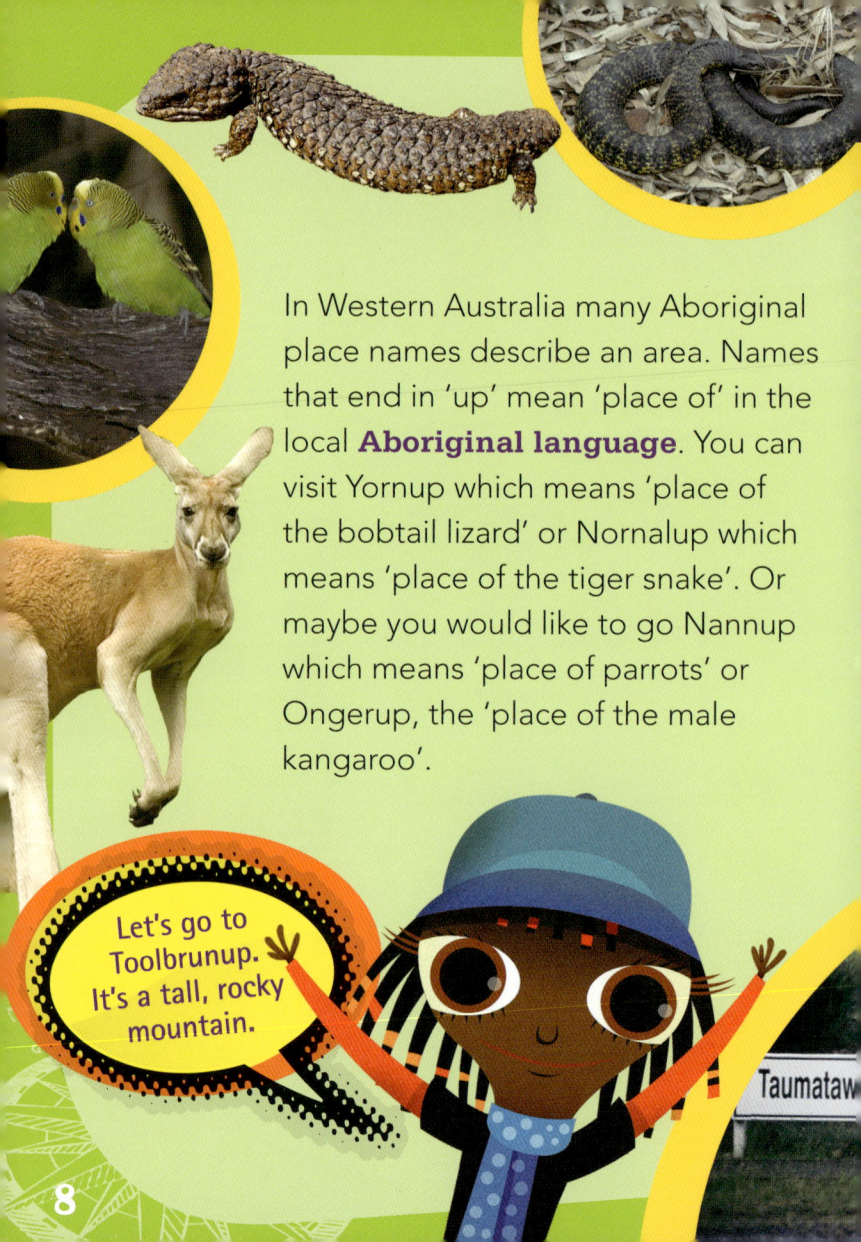

In Western Australia many Aboriginal place names describe an area. Names that end in 'up' mean 'place of' in the local **Aboriginal language**. You can visit Yornup which means 'place of the bobtail lizard' or Nornalup which means 'place of the tiger snake'. Or maybe you would like to go Nannup which means 'place of parrots' or Ongerup, the 'place of the male kangaroo'.

Let's go to Toolbrunup. It's a tall, rocky mountain.

Taumatawhakatangihangakoauauotamateaturipukakapikimaungahoronukupokaiwhenuakitanatahu is in New Zealand. In Maori it means: 'The place where Tamatea, the man with the big knees, who slid, climbed, and swallowed mountains, known as land eater, played his flute to his loved one'.

In the USA, 27 states have Native American names. 'Michigan' means 'great water' and 'Idaho' means 'sunrise, it is morning'.

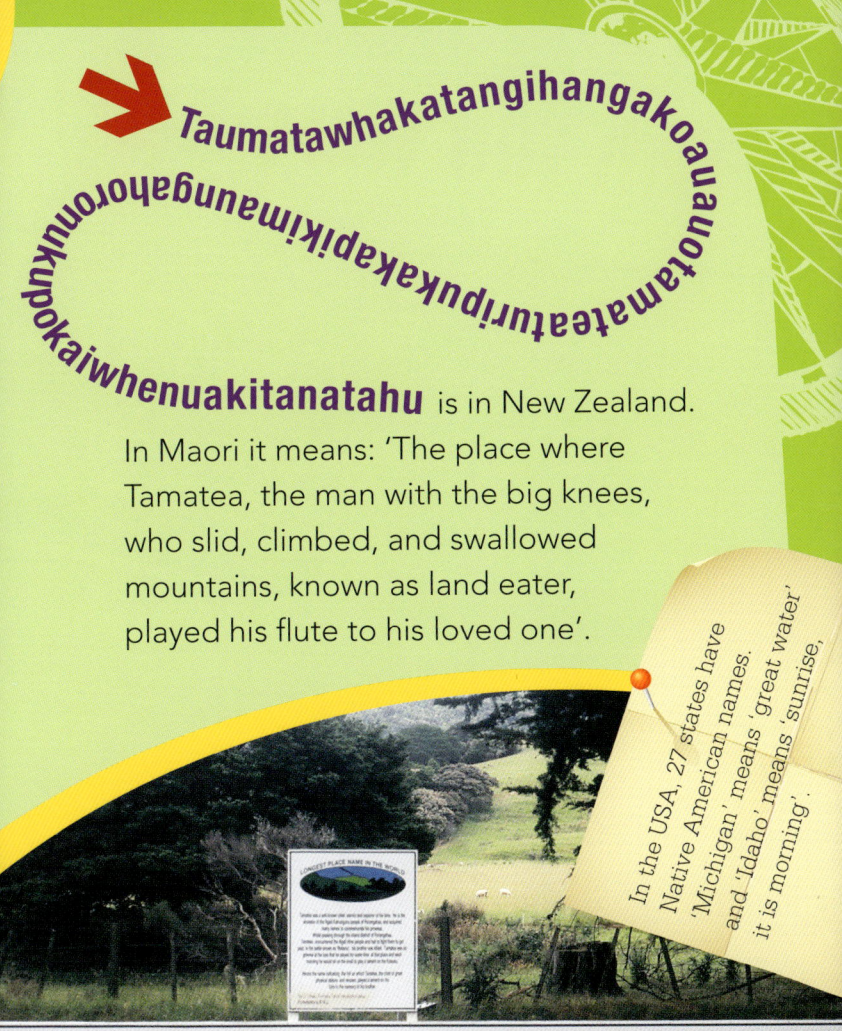

Wish You Were Here!

Woolloomooloo

In Sydney, Australia, there's a place called Woolloomooloo. Its name may come from the Aboriginal place name Waalamool. Some people think the name comes from 'Wool for the Looms of Old England', from the bales of wool sent to the UK in the 1860s.

Easter Island

Easter Island, in the Pacific Ocean, was given its name by the first European visitor, who arrived on Easter Sunday, 1722.

Santa Claus

One night, some people living in Arizona, USA, held a meeting to decide on a name for their town. During the meeting, a stranger came to the door in a sleigh. The children cried, "It's Santa Claus!" That's how the town of Santa Claus got its name!

Mosquito Coast

The Mosquito Coast around the Caribbean Sea is not called after the stinging insect. It is named for the Miskito – or Mosquito – the people of nearby Nicaragua.

Where Am I?

Many places in the world have the same name. It can be quite confusing – although in the USA it does tell you where the early **European settlers** came from. In the state of Maine there are towns named Poland, Sweden, Denmark, Wales and Norway. In New York State there is another Poland, as well as Italy, Greece and Rome!

I'm very confused because the USA states of California and Wyoming are names of towns too!

San Francisco, USA

Named After...

Many cities of the world are named after people who lived long ago.

Melbourne, Australia, was named after Lord Melbourne. He first became British Prime Minister in 1834.

Washington is the capital city of the USA. It was named after George Washington, the first President of the USA.

The city of São Paulo in Brazil was named after Saint Paul and the American city of San Francisco was named after Saint Francis.

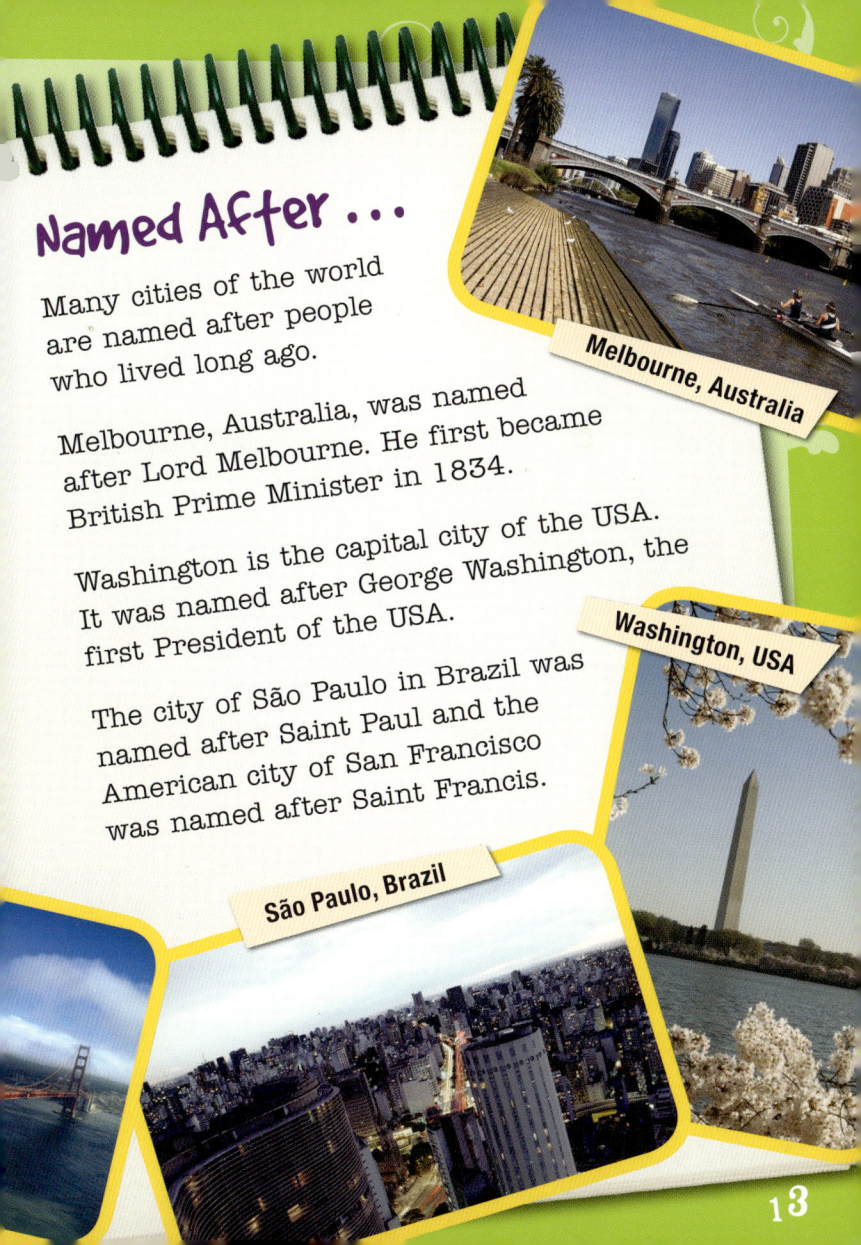

Melbourne, Australia

Washington, USA

São Paulo, Brazil

Say What?

Some place names are very hard to say! See if you can say these names quickly!

→ **Tzintzuntzan – say zin-zoon-zan**
It means the 'Place of the Hummingbirds'.
It's a city in Mexico.

→ **Aotearoa – say ow-tear-wa**
This is the Maori name for New Zealand.
It means 'Land of the Long White Cloud'.

→ **Zzyzx – say zeye-zix**
It's a settlement in California, USA.

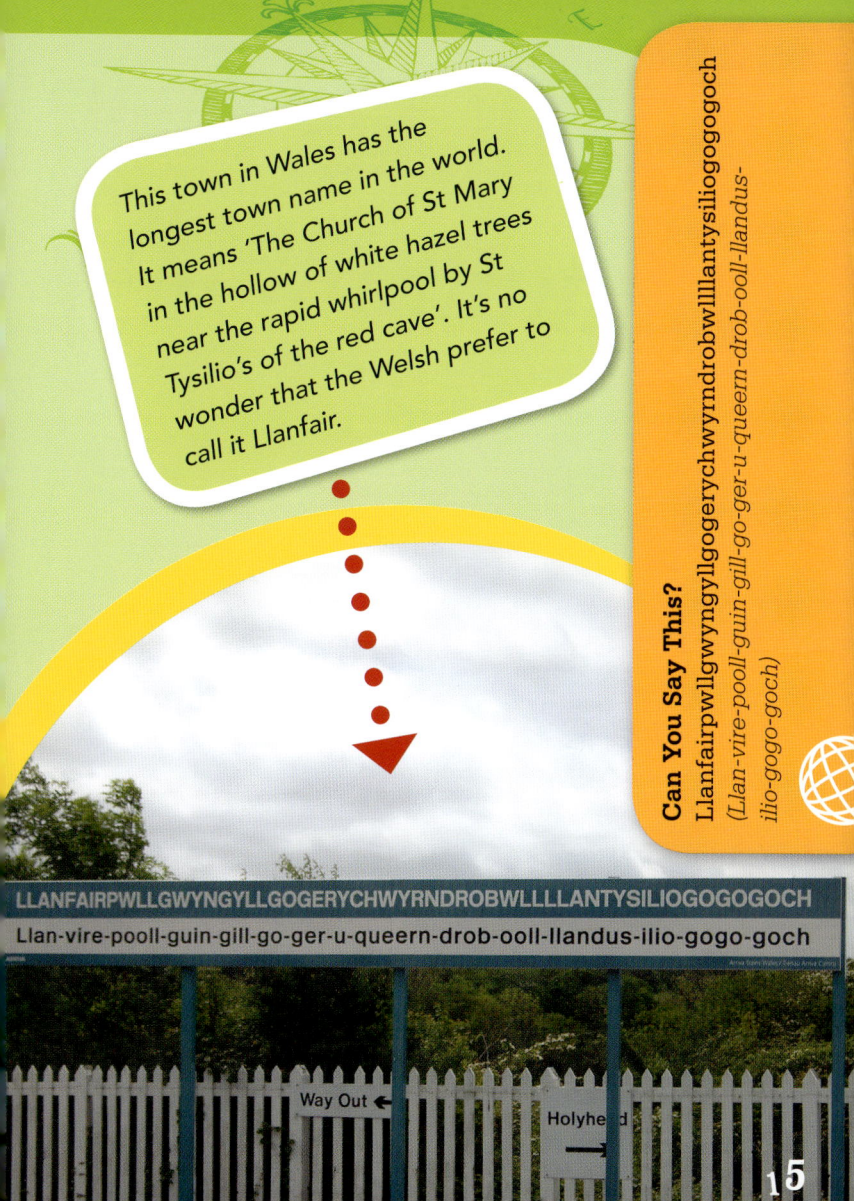

This town in Wales has the longest town name in the world. It means 'The Church of St Mary in the hollow of white hazel trees near the rapid whirlpool by St Tysilio's of the red cave'. It's no wonder that the Welsh prefer to call it Llanfair.

Can You Say This?
Llanfairpwllgwyngyllgogerychwyrndrobwllllantysiliogogogoch
(Llan-vire-pooll-guin-gill-go-ger-u-queern-drob-ooll-llandus-ilio-gogo-goch)

VERY Strange Names!

There are some very strange place names in the world.

In Australia there are three towns named after fruits: Orange, Berri and Banana. In **Orange** they grow cherries and in **Berri** they grow oranges! (And they don't grow bananas in **Banana!**)

In Albania there's **Puke**, in Austria there's **Spital** and in Spain there's **Poo**. These names would be really weird if they were in English-speaking countries!

Silly!
If you're searching for Silly, you'll find it in Belgium. If you are looking for the Isles of Scilly, you'll find them just off the coast of Cornwall, England.

Step Carefully in FELLDOWNHEAD

NO Eating in HAM & SANDWICH

TWELVEHEADS Population: 12

You can visit these places in England!

Cat's Elbow
In Germany there's a village called Katzenelnbogen. It means 'elbow of a cat'.

STAY ALERT IN LITTLE SNORING

The official name of Bangkok, the capital city of Thailand, sounds something like this when spoken in English:

Krung Thep Mahanakhon
Amon Rattanakosin Mahinthara
Ayuthaya Mahadilok Phop
Noppharat Ratchathani Burirom
Udomratchaniwet Mahasathan Amon
Piman Awatan Sathit Sakkathattiya
Witsanukam Prasit

Bangkok's also called the 'Happy City' and the 'City of Angels'. That sounds heavenly!

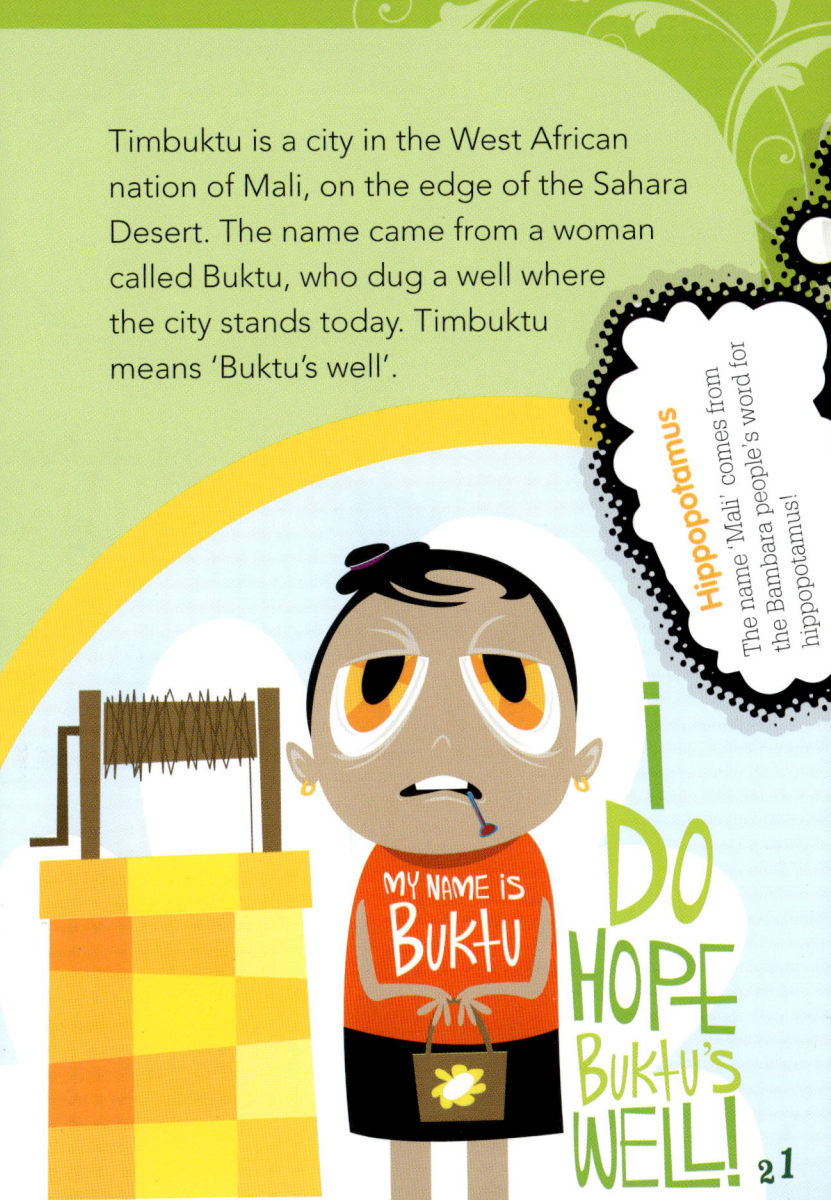

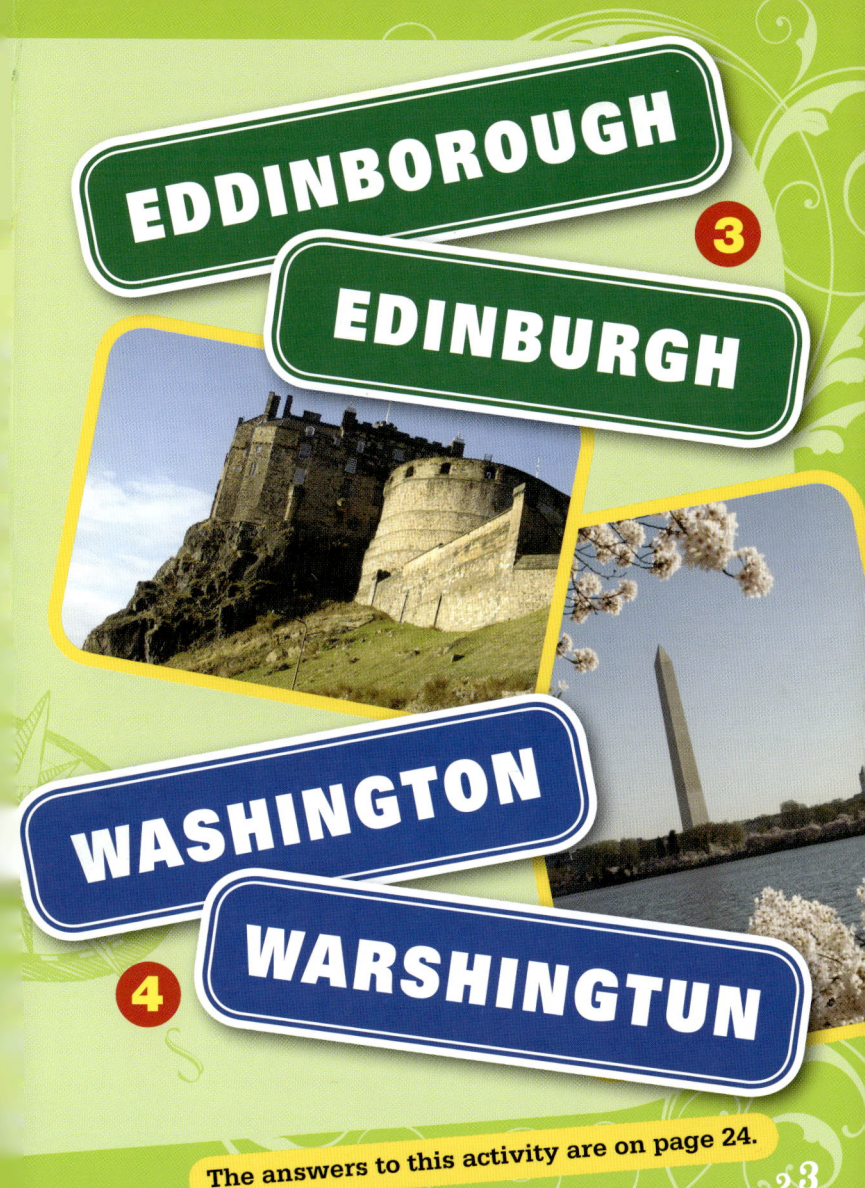

EDDINBOROUGH

3

EDINBURGH

WASHINGTON

4

WARSHINGTUN

The answers to this activity are on page 24.

23